GW00402336

Jesus calls

English text: Liam Kelly, Anne White
Original text: Albert Hari - Charles Singer

Illustrations: Mariano Valsesia - Betti Ferrero

CHAPTER 1 • *The first friends*   2

CHAPTER 2 • *The Twelve*   8

CHAPTER 3 • *Unwelcome*   14

CHAPTER 4 • *The rich young man*   20

CHAPTER 5 • *A demanding road*   26

INSIGHTS • *At the time of Jesus*   32

The first friends

Fra Angelico (1400-1455)
Decorated letter from the Missal
The Call of St Peter and St Andrew
(ms.558 fol.13v°)

Fra Angelico was a monk
in Florence, Italy.
He painted to decorate his monastery
and help his fellow monks to pray.
This illuminated 'O'
makes a perfect frame.
What moment of the call of Peter and
Andrew is he trying to imagine ?

© Orsi Battaglini-Giraudon / Museo di San Marco, Florence (Italy)

At the lakeside

View over Nazareth

For 30 years Jesus lived in Nazareth. One day he decides to go, leaving his family, his friends, his village. Why ? He knows that he is called to work far beyond his own little village.

About 30 kilometres east of Nazareth are the clear waters of Lake Tiberias, teeming with fish. Jesus sees the fishermen busy with their boats and their nets and stops to speak with them.

He invites the fishermen to follow him and to share his work. The four he calls are brothers from two different families: Simon and his brother Andrew, James and his brother John.

*Lake Tiberias is also called the Lake of Gennesaret or the Sea of Galilee. It lies between the green hills of Galilee and the desert peaks of Syria, and is 21kms long and 12kms wide.

Lake Tiberius

About forty years later

Mark wrote his gospel about the year 65 in Rome. At this time Simon (whom Jesus named Peter) and James had already been put to death for following Jesus. Mark had not been present at the lakeside, but it might have been Peter who told him how his first meeting with Jesus changed his life. He had been a simple fisherman, until Jesus invited him to become a "fisher of men and women".

A fisherman from Sri Lanka

3

Come with me

The Gospel according to Mark, chapter 1, verses 14 to 20.

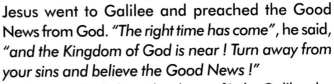

Jesus went to Galilee and preached the Good News from God. *"The right time has come"*, he said, *"and the Kingdom of God is near ! Turn away from your sins and believe the Good News !"*
As Jesus walked along the shore of Lake Galilee, he saw two fishermen, Simon and his brother Andrew, catching fish with a net. Jesus said to them, *"Come with me, and I will teach you to catch people."* At once they left their nets and went with him.

He went a little farther on and saw two other brothers, James and John, the sons of Zebedee. They were in their boat getting their nets ready. As soon as Jesus saw them, he called them; and they left their father Zebedee in the boat with the hired men and went with Jesus.

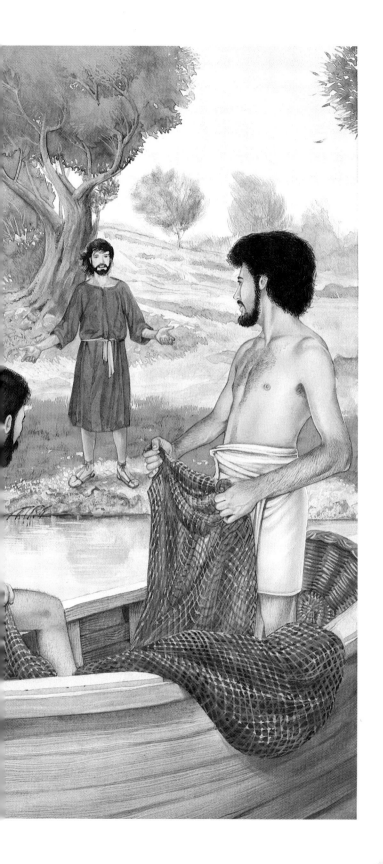

Kingdom of God

In Jesus's day this phrase made people think of a time when everyone would be happy, living by God's word. The Gospel does not explain the Kingdom (or Reign) of God, it describes it. It is like a seed, like yeast. It has already begun yet it is still to come in its fullness.

Good News

In Greek the word Gospel (euaggelion) means Good News. It is the announcement that God is coming to make people happy for ever. Jesus announces the Good News to the poor. His apostles are sent to bring this news to the whole world. The four gospels (Matthew, Mark, Luke and John) are books of the Good News.

Zebedee

This is a fine name. In Hebrew it is pronounced *"Zabday"* and means *"gift from God"*. In English we would say *"God-given"*.

The call to his followers

The day is coming

The day is coming when you will have to leave your family, the close circle where you feel at home and loved. The day is coming when you will have to launch out and live your own life. The day is coming when you have to leave in order to create, to invent, to start things for yourself.

The mission of Jesus

The day came when Jesus realised that he must leave his family and his village, to begin the mission which his Father had entrusted to him : to proclaim God's love for everyone.

Call

When you need someone to undertake a special job, to carry out a mission, you "call" them by name. *"Come on … ! We need you and your skills to share in this great mission. Do you want to be part of it ?"*

Response

Anyone who is called to a special task feels challenged. They wonder: Can I do this ? Is it really me you want ? They think about it and then respond, *"Well, if you have called me, here I am !"*

Together

The work to which Jesus calls people is immense and challenging. It can seem daunting, but you are not called on your own. All those who have been called can encourage and help one another. Everyone's efforts can be pooled together. Their energy, their faith and their enthusiasm have the strength to move mountains !

Those who say yes

They are all ages,
women, men and children.
They are from near and far:
workers, artists, students, the
unemployed, rich and poor,
powerful and ordinary.
They come from all corners of the
world to work together.

The call of Jesus has reached them,
touching their hearts and minds,
changing their lives.

They have decided to respond to
Jesus' call, to believe in him,
and to entrust themselves
completely to him.

They have decided
to follow Jesus Christ,
such as they are,
big or small, sinners or just,
brave or weak -
and to go with him,
no matter how difficult
the road may be,
to accomplish the mission
that Jesus entrusts to them:
to announce the love of God
to the ends of the earth !

CHAPTER 2

The Twelve

Fra Angelico (1400-1455)
Sermon on the Mount
(after restoration)

Another Fra Angelico
painting but in a very
different style from
the one on page 2.
Would you know it was
the same artist ?
Which painting might
help you to pray ?

© Orsi Battaglini - Giraudon / Museo di San Marco, Florence (Italy)

They followed Jesus

Sculpture of Peter in the church of St Peter in Rome, Italy

Jesus did not work alone. He called a group of twelve, (the number of the twelve tribes of Israel). The number signifies wholeness. These twelve are called to stay with Jesus and then to be sent out. The leader of the group is Peter. Judas is in charge of the money. The Twelve stay with Jesus until his arrest.

The Twelve were not alone. There was a larger group of 72 disciples with them which is often forgotten. Jesus included a group of women among his followers. This would have been unusual at that time.*

The work continued

Jesus was betrayed by Judas, one of the Twelve. When Jesus was arrested all the others ran away.

After his death and resurrection, they regained their courage. They came to understand in a new way what his presence ("being with him") and mission ("being sent by him") meant. They were to carry the Good News to the ends of the earth.

The example of new apostles, like Paul, encouraged them to be even bolder in proclaiming the Good News. The women played an important role in welcoming groups of Christians to their homes. When the Christian communities, retold the story of the call of the Twelve, they could see that they too were continuing the mission for which the Twelve had been prepared.

Statue of Mary Magdalen at Lestelle-Betharam, in France

*Among the women who followed Jesus and are spoken of in the Gospel, we can mention: "Mary of Magdala, Joanna, wife of Chuza, Susanna and others"(Luke 8:2-3), "Mary the mother of Jesus and his mother's sister" (John 19:25), "many women who had followed Jesus from Galilee... Mary, mother of James and Joseph, and the mother of the sons of Zebedee."(Matthew 27: 55-56).

He calls the Twelve

The Gospel according to Mark, chapter 3, verses 13 to 19.

Jesus went up a hill and called to himself the men he wanted. They came to him, and he chose twelve, whom he named apostles, "I have chosen you to be with me," he told them. "I will also send you out to preach, and you will have authority to drive out demons."

These are the twelve he chose:

Simon (Jesus gave him the name Peter);

James and his brother John,

the sons of Zebedee

(Jesus gave them the name Boanerges,

which means "Men of Thunder");

Andrew,

Philip,

Bartholomew,

Matthew,

Thomas,

James son of Alphaeus,

Thaddeus,

Simon the Patriot,

and Judas Iscariot, who betrayed Jesus.

What do the names of the twelve apostles mean ?

Simon : God has answered
Peter : Rock
John : God has graced
James : He will take charge.
Andrew : Courageous
Philip : Lover of horses
Bartholomew : Son of Ptolomy
Matthew : Gift of God
Thomas : Twin
James, son of Alphaeus : James, son of the cattle farmer
Thaddeus (Jude) : Gift of God
Simon the Patriot : Simon the freedom-fighter
Judas Iscariot : The man from Kariot, the land of ravines, (near Hebron)

Why Twelve ?

Twelve is not just a random number. It has a deeper meaning. It signifies completeness. There were twelve tribes in Israel. There are twelve months in the year. Jesus chose twelve apostles.

Mission

Team...

It is impossible to succeed in any big project without gathering a team. The team members put into practice the plans that are decided on. They dedicate themselves completely to the work.

...variety

The strength of a team and its ability to be creative come from its different members. Different ideas are needed, different characters, different minds, backgrounds, ways of going about things. So the skills of each person will help the task to be completed.

Unique

Each person has their own special place in the team. Their talent, their know-how makes them irreplaceable because they are unique. In a team each one plays a part which is theirs alone.

Mission

The team gathered together by Jesus is made up of all those who answer his call and who put his word into practice. To that team – the Church - Jesus entrusts the mission of proclaiming the Good News of God's love.

Apostles and Disciples

Everyone is called to be an apostle, that is to say someone sent, a messenger. Each person, with the gifts of their body and spirit, is called by Jesus to be an apostle, his envoy, his messenger sent to make God's love visible for everyone.

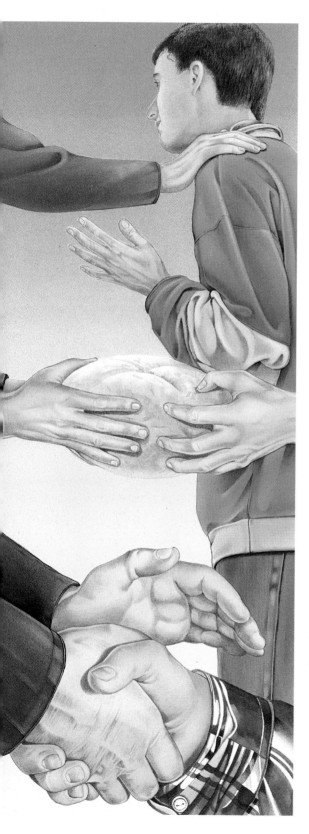

Still counting !

How many apostles !
All over the world
they are answering Jesus' call.

What do they do today ?
They forgive those who do wrong.
They reveal the power of gentleness.
They love God and their neighbours
with a love that
overcomes everything.

What do they do today ?
They hold out healing hands.
They remove the poison of jealousy.
They break bread together.
They pray to their Father in heaven
and offer happiness to all
God's children on earth.

Would you like to add your name
to the long list of today's apostles ?

CHAPTER 3

Unwelcome

Paolo Caliari
also known as
Veronese.
(1528-1588)
The Banquet at
Levi's house

The artist has pictured
Levi's dinner party in the
richness of his own
century. All the characters
in the painting seem to
have lots to attract their
attention, but at the centre
of all this Jesus and Levi
are deep in conversation.

© Giraudon - Private Collection, Paris (France)

It's a scandal !

Customs officers and tax collectors (often called *publicans*) were very unpopular in Israel. People accused them of getting rich illegally, of demanding more in taxes than the State required and of pocketing the difference for themselves. The Pharisees blamed them for having contact with the pagans and so making themselves impure. They were treated like sinners.

Jesus' behaviour was surprising. He called a customs officer, Levi, son of Alphaeus, to follow him. Levi organised a meal at home with his publican friends, and invited Jesus and his disciples. The scribes of the Pharisee group said it was a scandal : *"You don't eat with those sort of people !"* Jesus explains his action : *"I have not come to call good people, but sinners."*

A woman making bread in Egypt

A real welcome

Harvesting tea-leaves in Sri Lanka

After the death and resurrection of Jesus, Christians used to come together to eat, to pray and to remember Jesus. Soon problems arose. The rich took the best places and the poor were left to one side. Some Jewish Christians refused to share the meal with non-Jewish Christians.

The example of Jesus, who ate with publicans and sinners, helped the first Christians to understand that they were called to welcome everybody around the same table.

In God's sight, people are neither Jew nor pagan, slave nor free.

A villager offering bread in Romania

* *The people of Jesus' time were hit by many taxes. For the Roman empire they paid land tax, people tax, road tax and taxes on bridges and markets. The publicans were in charge of collecting this money. Besides this, the Jews paid a Temple tax and tithes (a tenth) on the land and any produce which they grew.*

Jesus and Levi

The Gospel according to Mark, chapter 2, verses 13 to 17.

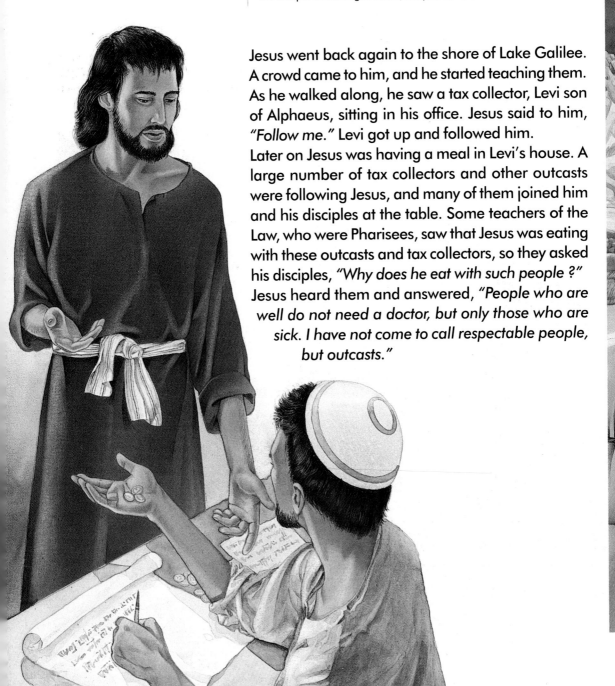

Jesus went back again to the shore of Lake Galilee. A crowd came to him, and he started teaching them. As he walked along, he saw a tax collector, Levi son of Alphaeus, sitting in his office. Jesus said to him, *"Follow me."* Levi got up and followed him.

Later on Jesus was having a meal in Levi's house. A large number of tax collectors and other outcasts were following Jesus, and many of them joined him and his disciples at the table. Some teachers of the Law, who were Pharisees, saw that Jesus was eating with these outcasts and tax collectors, so they asked his disciples, *"Why does he eat with such people ?"* Jesus heard them and answered, *"People who are well do not need a doctor, but only those who are sick. I have not come to call respectable people, but outcasts."*

Levi

The *"Levi"* of the scripture text is probably *"Matthew the publican"* (Mt 10:3) the author of the gospel which bears his name.

"Follow me !"

In the gospel, *"to follow someone"* does not just mean *"to walk behind someone"*. To follow Jesus means to be close to him, to share his life and deeds, to believe in him, to be ready to give your life for him.

Pharisees

The Pharisees were fanatical about Jewish law. They wanted to make it apply right down to the last detail. The Gospel often showed them up as being over-zealous and hypocritical.

Change

Goodness

No one, except Jesus Christ
is without sin. Being good means trying
to follow the example of Jesus, loving God as a Father
and our neighbours as brothers and sisters.

Sinner

Everyone is a sinner because we all give in to evil sometimes and do wrong. But no one need remain trapped forever in their sin. To be a sinner means turning away from the example of Jesus and living far from the love of God and neighbour.

Labels

It is easy to label some by calling them 'good' or 'evil'. Aren't we all sometimes good and sometimes bad ?

Change

Just because someone does wrong does not mean that they should be thought of as bad for ever ! Everyone, with God's help, is capable of change, of turning back. When evil appears attractive we can, with God's help, choose to say 'no' and turn away.

Not Rejected But Loved

Jesus rejects no one. He calls each person to turn from wrong and respond to his love. For God the Father, there is no such thing as a despised sinner. There are just children for whom God cares.

All
alike

Alike !
We are all the same.

One day
full of generosity
giving without counting,
and the next day
fired up with temper
and full of anger !

One day
my lips bear
the sun's own smile,
and then on another day
my mouth spits out
mocking words
which slice deeper than a knife.

All alike:
we are good
and we are sinners !

God trusts everyone.
God trusts me
and never stops giving me
the chance
to live in the light,
of God's love
and truth !

CHAPTER 4

The rich young man

Painted mural of Christ in the monastery of Eski Gümüs, Turkey

Can you imagine looking up at this painting high on the dome or wall of a great church ? How different is it from painting or statues of Jesus in churches you know ?

© F. Zvardon

A newcomer

Young Palestinian on a donkey

Lots of people were following Jesus. Some had left everything to be with him. Peter, Andrew and John left their little fishing business, Levi abandoned his work at the tax desk. Others travelled great distances from their homes, their families, their villages. Some were poor, with neither possessions, jobs nor families.

One day a young man rushed up to Jesus and said *"What must I do to win eternal life ?"* When he told Jesus that he already kept the commandments, Jesus suggested he could do more: *"Sell your possessions and give the money to the poor !"* The young man bowed his head and went off sad. He was too attached to his wealth.

Statue from the Israel Museum in Jerusalem.

The first Christians and the poor

Mark told this story to the rich and poor Christians in his community. What is the point of the story ?

- That Jesus loves them too, just as he loved the man who rushed up to him.
- That Jesus is asking them to keep the commandments and suggesting that they go further.
- Some Christians had already sold their goods and shared the money with the poor.* The joy of sharing is worth more than the sadness of everyone looking after themselves.

Carrying bricks in Nepal.

* The Acts of the Apostles which recounts the life of the first Christians says: "All those who had become believers were united and held everything in common." (Acts 2:44)

Jesus loved him

Gospel according to Mark, chapter 10, verses 17 to 22.

As Jesus was starting on his way again, a man ran up, knelt before him, and asked him, *"Good Teacher, what must I do to receive eternal life ?"*

"Why do you call me good ?" Jesus asked him. *"No one is good except God alone. You know the commandments: 'Do not commit murder; do not commit adultery; do not steal; do not accuse anyone falsely; do not cheat; respect your father and your mother.'"*

"Teacher," the man said, *"ever since I was young, I have obeyed all these commandments."*

Jesus looked straight at him with love and said, *"You need only one thing. Go and sell all you have and give the money to the poor, and you will have riches in heaven; then come and follow me."* When the man heard this, gloom spread over his face, and he went away sad, because he was very rich.

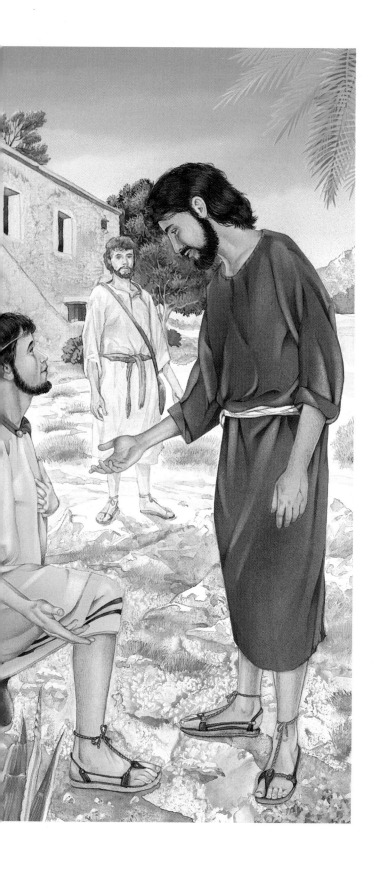

Good Teacher

The young man addressed Jesus as 'good'. Jesus reminded him that it was only God who was to be called 'good'.

Commandments

The *ten commandments* are the heart of the Law of Moses which faithful Jews observe.

He went away

Jesus never forces anyone. Everyone is free to follow him or to go their own way.

Decisions

Riches

We are rich if we have all we wish for and do not have to worry about tomorrow…We are rich if we have the chance to meet lots of people, to have friends and be loved, to have many skills and qualities… To be rich is not a bad thing. It is a great responsibility.

Attached to Wealth

Jesus does not reject rich people. He never rejects anyone ! He simply warns them of the danger of ending up prisoners, of the wealth they possess.
What might be holding us prisoner ?

To follow Jesus…

How can we truly follow Jesus if we are imprisoned in any way ?

…Wholeheartedly

It's the road of love that people take with Jesus. On that road people share; they do not just look after themselves. On that road, with Jesus, people do not just give a bit; they give wholeheartedly !

Free to choose

Jesus leaves everyone free to choose: to accept or refuse to go further, to share or to keep selfishly. But, whichever decision is made, Christ's love for each person is unchanging.

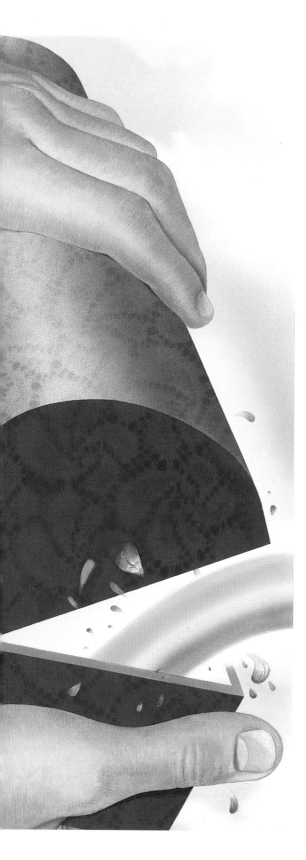

Treasures

What priceless treasures
you possess:
the goodness of your heart,
the joy of your smile,
the skills of your hands
and your intelligence !
Will you share them generously ?

What riches you possess !

What about the words
from your lips !
Will you use them
to defend those
who are persecuted ?

What about the strength
of your courage !
Will you use it to lift up
those who fall
under the weight of sorrow ?

What about the happiness
of your life !
Will you use it
to surround with light
those who lose their way
in the night of worry ?

What treasures you have !
Will you offer them
in following
Christ Jesus ?

CHAPTER 5

A demanding road

Decorated letter 'D' from the Missal: Entrance into Jerusalem, c.1500

Another example of an illuminated letter from a prayer book. This is from the 16th century. There is much more detail than in the 'O' (page 2). What event in the life of Jesus is pictured here ?

© Bridgeman-Giraudon / Wallace Collection, London (England)

Knowing where you are going

The Roman Colosseum in Italy

People followed Jesus for lots of reasons. Some people thought he would overthrow the Romans.* They were hoping for a good place in the Kingdom that Jesus proclaimed. Jesus did not mislead them. He told them that it would not always be easy and they would have to carry the cross daily.

Jesus prepared to go up to Jerusalem, where he would face the civic and religious leaders. These people did not agree with his message. To go up to Jerusalem was to risk his life. Eventually he will be crucified. Will those who have begun to answer his call follow him right to the end ?

Remembering the words of Jesus

There are some words which renew our courage. A long time later, when the early Christians read the words of Jesus in the gospel of Luke, they had a better understanding of the difficulties

Bridge in Carpates, Romania

they faced because of the Gospel: separation from their family, having to travel to spread the Good News, and the problems of daily life.

Statue of a Roman soldier on the Victor Emmanuel Bridge in Rome, Italy

* At the time of Jesus, his country was occupied by Roman legions. Pontius Pilate, a representative of the Emperor, controlled all the country. Many people in Jesus' day were hoping to be set free.

27

B i b l e

Carrying your cross

Gospel according to Luke, chapter 9, verses 57 to 61 and 23.

As they went on their way, a man said to Jesus, *"I will follow you wherever you go."* Jesus said to him, *"Foxes have holes, and birds have nests, but the Son of Man has nowhere to lie down and rest."*...

Someone else said, *"I will follow you, sir; but first let me go and say good-bye to my family."*

Jesus said to him, *"Anyone who starts to plough and then keeps looking back is of no use to the Kingdom of God."*...

And he said to them all, *"Anyone who wants to come with me must forget self, take up their cross every day, and follow me."*

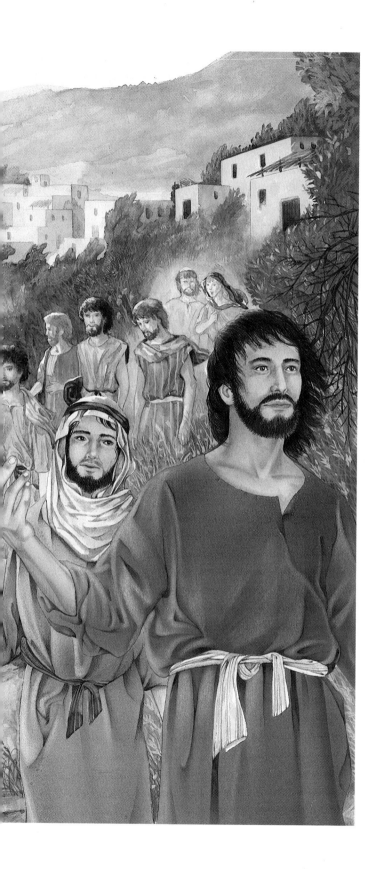

On the road

After leaving his village of Nazareth, Jesus travelled all around the country. He was always on the road. When people heard his words and saw what he did, many of them wanted to follow him.

Son of Man

This phrase recalls a vision from the prophet Daniel (about 175 BC). He describes the coming of a Son of Man on the clouds of heaven to save from judgement those who were his own. The first Christians understood that Jesus is the Son of Man who was to come at the end of time.

Cross

The cross was seen as an instrument of terrible and humiliating torture. From the start, many could not understand Jesus's crucifixion. Gradually the followers of Jesus understood that like him they too had to "carry their cross" every day.

The way of Jesus

Leader

Jesus is not just a revolutionary or a philosopher with new ideas. Nor is he a teacher thinking up interesting theories.

Jesus is the saviour coming to free people from all that imprisons them. Jesus is the Son of God coming to teach people to live in the love of God and their neighbours.

Life's road...

Those who decide to follow Jesus choose a path which will change their lives.

Jesus leads them along a road where they will share with each other, give to one another and believe in God and in each other.

...a difficult road

The road to which Jesus calls his friends is hard. Jesus asks them to give up being self-centred, to leave pride behind, to stop being small-minded, to carry the burden of others, to believe in him without seeing him...

...a new road

The road to which Jesus calls is completely new ! It is a road where you pray for your enemies, where you always pardon, where you share without counting the cost, where you place yourself completely into the hands of God the Father.

...of love

Jesus calls us to love ! Nothing else ! Jesus proclaims and shows people that only love is able to transform the world into a kingdom where all are equal children of God.

On the way

They set out on the road
with the unforgettable
words of Jesus
singing in their hearts
and in their lives.

They set out,
opening their arms
to those who are wounded
by daily worries and fears.
They set out to offer
the daily gift of kindness.

The unforgettable words of Jesus,
burn like flames of fire in their memory.
And these words are a daily call,
urging them to continue on earth
the work of love and of peace,
which the Lord Jesus began
when he gave his life
to save the world !

At the time of Jesus

The country (see map on page 35)

It is a small poor country. From Nazareth to Jerusalem it is only 114 kms. The country has been occupied by Roman troops since 63BC. It's a land with a long history, at the crossroads of civilisation and continents.

The regions

In the north, Galilee has a pleasant climate, with charming villages and a clear water lake. In the centre is the hilly region of Samaria. The inhabitants of this region, the Samaritans, are shunned by their neighbours. In the south is Judea, a mountainous region, partly desert, with a harsh climate.

Jerusalem, the ruins of a synagogue

The towns

The Roman and Jewish authorities have their headquarters in Jerusalem, the capital. It is the religious centre of the country because the Temple is there. Jesus was crucified in Jerusalem. Bethlehem, the ancient city of David, is, according to the evangelists, the birthplace of Jesus. However, he spent the largest part of his life in Nazareth, a little village in Galilee. He began his public ministry in the Capernaum area, the town of the apostle Peter.

The Judean countryside

Geography

To the west lay the Mediterranean Sea, often called the "Great Sea". To the east the river Jordan flows in a deep valley through Lake Tiberias and south towards the Dead Sea, which in Jesus's day was called the "Salt Sea".

The country can be divided into four strips, each parallel to the sea.

1   A coastal plain narrowing towards the north.
2   A mountain chain where some peaks are over 1000 metres. It is desert-like in the south, with rich valleys in the north.
3   The deepest trench in the world, the Jordan Valley. The surface of the Dead Sea is about 400 metres below sea level.
4   Various plateaus beyond the Jordan. Certain peaks are more than 1200 metres high.

Today

The largest part of the country where Jesus lived now belongs to Israel and contains Palestinian self-governing territories. The neighbouring countries are Lebanon to the north, Syria and Jordan to the east, and Egypt to the south.

Lake Tiberius

The Junior Bible

The Junior Bible series brings you books to enjoy.
You will hear the story of Jesus
and his invitation to follow him.

You will learn about the customs,
people and places of Jesus's time
and how the Good News he brought is just as alive today.

You will not learn everything there is to know about Jesus
from this or any book,
but you can begin to discover
the wonder of Jesus as a friend and companion.

The country of Jesus

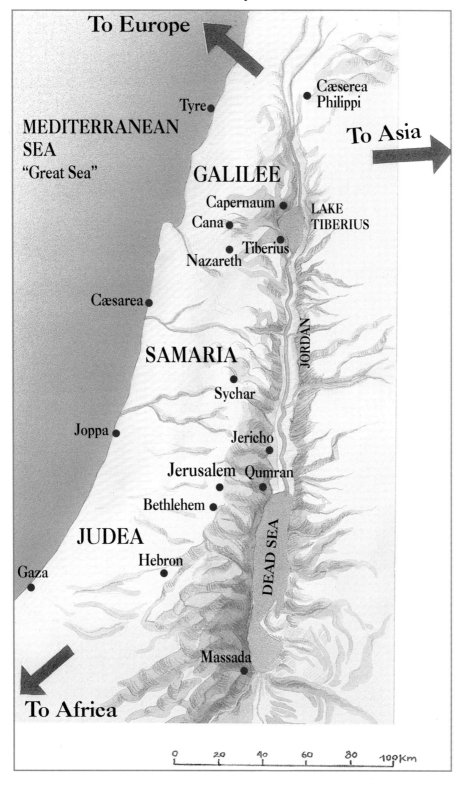

To Europe

Tyre

Cæserea
Philippi

MEDITERRANEAN
SEA
"Great Sea"

To Asia

GALILEE

Capernaum

Cana

LAKE
TIBERIUS

Tiberius

Nazareth

Cæsarea

JORDAN

SAMARIA

Sychar

Joppa

Jericho

Jerusalem   Qumran

Bethlehem

DEAD SEA

JUDEA

Hebron

Gaza

Massada

To Africa

0   20   40   60   80   100 Km

TEXTS

Liam KELLY - Anne WHITE

Albert HARI - Charles SINGER

PICTURE RESEARCH

Sandrine WINTER

PHOTOGRAPHY

Frantisek ZVARDON

Alsace MÉDIA

Patrice THÉBAULT

ILLUSTRATORS

Mariano VALSESIA

Betti FERRERO

MIA. Milan Illustrations Agency

LAYOUT

Studio Graphique B.BAYLE

Nihil obstat: George Stokes. censor
Imprimatur: Rt Rev Arthur Barrow VG
Brentwood 15 January 1998

MATTHEW JAMES PUBLISHING LTD
19 WELLINGTON CLOSE
CHELMSFORD, ESSEX CM1 2EE

ISBN 1 898366 41 1